The Magic of Knitting

Christopher James

Templar Poetry

First Published 2011 by Templar Poetry
Templar Poetry is an imprint of Delamide & Bell

Fenelon House
Kingsbridge Terrace
58 Dale Road, Matlock, Derbyshire
DE4 3NB
www.templarpoetry.co.uk

ISBN 978-1-906285-16-6

Typeset by Pliny
Printed and bound in India

To Noah

Acknowledgements

The Small Ghost of Soho was written and performed as part of the the Eric Gregory 50th anniversary celebrations in 2010, organised by Roddy Lumsden.

Charlotte Bronte in the Wild West was previous published in The Frogmore Papers.

Other titles from Christopher James include, *The Invention of Butterfly* (Ragged Raven Press, 2006) and *Farewell to the Earth* (Arc, 2011).

Thank you to Nick Keeble for inspiration for *When My Father Taught Us to Knit*.

Contents

The Manly Art of Knitting

When my father taught us to knit
he held the needles like fencing swords,
told us how Cary Grant never dropped
a stitch in *Mr Lucky*; we listened
to the clack of his pins, while watching
Ipswich Town come undone.

He'd show us crowds and corn fields:
immaculate rows of purl stitch, binding off
with stories of Captain Scott knitting
his way through the Antarctic winter.
In the evenings he reminisced
about old episodes of *Knit with Norbury*.

He carried his crochet hook like a penknife;
would think nothing of leaving the office
to fix a dropped stitch; he gave us
a copy each of *The Manly Art of Knitting*.
In spring, we threw ourselves into the surf
diving through loops of brown waves.

When we were bullied, he told us to think
about the big centre forward who knitted
the world's longest football scarf. That summer
he led us to Normandy, threw open the doors
to the great hall at Bayeux and cried:
'This, is this what you call women's work?'

Vanishing Trick

Supernova SN 1979C *was found after a massive*
cosmic explosion 31 years ago (1979) and may have
been the birth of the youngest ever black hole.

A star implodes and thirty years on
a black hole is born, like a long player
held up to the sun; in its warped grooves
pieces of 1979 spin around its edges:
an *I Hate Disco* sticker, my father's beard
and a cinema seat containing someone
watching *Star Trek: The Motion Picture.*
The year has collapsed on itself,
drawing everything in: luminous fragments
of punk rock; the tennis bat I launched
at the boy across the road, Sid Vicious
singing *My Way* and the fur lined coffin
containing the remains of John Wayne.
There are disco lights in the heavens
and at their centre, a point where there is
a darkness so complete, nothing,
not even light can escape.

Still in fields far from town you can
hear, faintly, Blondie's *Heart of Glass*
transmitting from the star's exhausted core.

A mining vessel crosses the Event Horizon
and fifty million light years away I am still
riding my bicycle on a Paisley estate.
My father is at work, my mother makes tea
and for thirty minutes snow falls on the Sahara.
Someone has hole-punched the universe
and my childhood has fallen through.
In this anomaly of time and space, the gravity
is so great that even the General Election
result is reversed; peering into its dark heart,
we imagine at its centre, a front room
with a television showing The Morecambe and Wise
Christmas Special; the year gleams in Eric's
glasses, then vanishes into Ernie's top hat.

The First Blonde in Space

For Martha

A day to go and you have outgrown
your capsule, the warm spaceship in which you spin
like Valentina Teshkova, the first blonde
in space, who traded wisecracks with Khrushchev.
We have seen you beamed in black and white
weightless, in the care of the motherland
as grainy as Soviet television.
Your profile is known to generations.
Now we wait for you to cross the abyss
and become the third star in our sky,
but when you parachute down, as one of us,
you will not forget this loneliness.
Thousands gather and when you emerge,
you are, for a moment, the newest thing on Earth.

The Beautiful Friendship

We wanted the house on St. Botolph's Street,
the yellow one, with the blue bicycle outside.
On the table was a copy of *Dark Star Safari*
and a candle flickering from a good Bordeaux.

Two months later and we're round for dinner:
king prawns, with fresh chillies and lime.
Afterwards I take off their cupboard door
with my impersonation of Brendan Behan.

The girls got on; I swatted up on my Theroux
and soon got the measure of the man.
We went over on Fridays and played
on a chess set of the Thirties poets.

I usually played white; Auden, of course,
was my Queen, MacNeice the king.
He would pit Spender against Day-Lewis
and sacrifice Betjeman for my Stevie Smith.

That summer, we camped on the South Coast
and chartered a yacht on the Solent.
We cooked pork in Pernod and took turns
to recite Shakespeare's sonnets from the prow.

After the sinking we swam back to shore,
took off in their maroon Triumph Dolomite
and headed back to town; only then did I use
my key for the house on St. Botolph's Street.

The Calcutta Roller Skating Club

In sixteen different colours of Lycra,
a garland of flowers around each
of our necks we skate through the streets
like electrons flowing through
the City of Furious Creative Energy.
On our iPods are the new sounds
of Moheener, Bhoomi and Bhangra Hip Hop.
We know all the moves: the double pirouette,
the reverse turkey and the nutcracker splits.
In line, we limbo beneath the barrier
at the United Bank of India. We emerge
through the Monsoon in mid air
doing the helicopter, the high ostrich;
spinning like marbles spilt across the floor.
When we get tired, we pick up tows
from yellow metered taxis.
Not for us the blade or bicycle.
We are the free workers of the call centre,
the fruit market and the high rise.
We light up the city like a malfunction
at the West Bengal State Electricity Board.
We eat on the go, bowls of fish curry,
samosas and Coca-Cola; indigestion is common.
When we crash, we do it well,
like Maksood Salam, who went clean

through the double glass doors
of the Institute of Management.
You will know us by tracks we leave
on the greens of the Royal Calcutta Golf Club.
and the jet trails above the Indian Ocean.
We are the upwardly mobile; the future now:
a silent carnival of snaking light.

The Flat Earthers

I awoke on the flat Earth,
all the world a piece of unleavened bread.
On the balls of my feet, I reached a town
where the people knew their minds
but refused to acknowledge a horizon.
No one would sell me an orange – at least not whole.
To divide the fruit was to deny the sphere.
Old horses pulled sleighs through the dust.
Wise men spoke of the end of the world.
They danced flat-footed and droned
in the flat vowels of the Midlands.
The world is a like a bullring, they told me.
We are the matadors who kick up
the golden earth – there is a single exit
and a single entrance, but no above or below.
Think of it this way, said another,
we are dancers on a tabletop, tapping
out our steps for the master's pleasure.
Donkey's grazed in thin pastures;
children played with Frisbees and spinning tops.
University degrees were given flat not rolled.
I can see, they said, that you do not believe
that we live on a disk spinning through time
like a plate thrown at a wedding.
Your eyes betray you; you do not think
the sun is propped up on wooden stakes

like a photograph on a mantle-piece.
I suppose you believe in the Ying and Yang
and that men travelled in ships to the moon?
I walked until the sun slipped away
and I found a man in a flat cap,
heaving old Mercedes and rusting Bentleys
off the edge of the world,
watching them drift into space.

Landing on the Earth

We step, my daughter and I,
like Armstrong and Aldrin
into the white dust of a blue moon.
From the backdoor, into the cosmos,
we are already ankle-deep.
Our garden is unknown; we are
wary visitors, respectful of its strange silence.
Trees bowed, the shed hushed,
there are soft craters where the grass
has worn away beneath the swing.
Icicles point their fingers at the ground
and we make our snowman in the dark.
We go about our work, roaming apart,
knowing the other is close by.
We scoop handfuls, pressing
and sculpting, buttoning his coat with ivy.
My son's tricycle is a dune buggy
doubled with a drift inches deep.
Behind us, our house rises like
the lunar module, and in orbit, my son
is Michael Collins, his face pressed
against the glass. He calls:
'Are you alright, Dad? I can see you.'
'Are you alright?' And above us,
the moon shines as brightly
as an Earth entirely covered in snow.

Tank Crew

Limping back, like a beetle half-crushed,
the tank unwinds towards us; the crew leaps
from its dented shell, wild-eyed from the fury.
Beached on this desert of dragonflies and ravens,
the tank steams; a lizard scuttles from its heat.
Our hands are bloodied with oil; theirs with blood.
They ask what they can do; they want to return.
But the tank is wrecked, charred; a steel tomb.
They pick up my tools, not knowing what they are.
Sleeves at our elbows, we work beneath the sun's
slow arc; they cheer each clank and misfire.

Sucking at their canteens, they chatter madly,
like a soccer team at half time; only the commander
is calm; he combs his hair and narrows his eyes
to the horizon, as if waiting while we check his oil.
Together we will it back into life. Then each one
climbs in; the radio operator is last, a wishbone
clamped to his head, thinking now only
of his machine gun. I watch them caterpillar away
into the dunes and hollows of the desert.
I do not see them again, although I wait until night
when the sky is speckled with a rust of stars.

The Pilot Officer

Most of the time he drank tea,
skimmed old Polish papers
or hummed *Hej Sokoly*.
He complimented my mother
on her housekeeping, leant over
to smell the fresh lilies
she brought in from the fields
or listened quietly to Mr Churchill
speaking on the wireless.
The pilot officer would eat his tea,
smile as my mother's fingers
read the piano or pray as Connie
held open the family Bible.
I could place both of my shoes
inside one of his leather boots.
While I was at school, he would
flip his plane across the skies,
like a stick thrown at a Chestnut tree
and once, on a day trip
to Walton-on-the-Naze
he put his arm around me
as we walked along the front.
Only once did he go to his room,
dress in his full uniform and try
to hang himself by his pale blue tie.
The children played in the garden
while the ambulance drove away.
But most of the time he drank tea.

The Matador Maestro

He played the bull like he played the violin,
each pass a noble sweep of the bow.
We marvelled at the *verónica*, how he turned
on his heel and brought us, astonished, to our feet.
Barely twenty, the toast of all of Spain, Manuel Grenero
a lean, gold figure, like a beam of sunlight in the ring.

In the evenings he drank sangria and horchata,
and played *corridos* in the cafés of Madrid,
old folk songs for passers-by, his matador's cloak
spread out to catch the pesetas.,
He waited, in the vibrato of the heat haze
for Pocapena, his final bull. Flung high, he heard
the sonatas of Enrique Granados, the music of the Spanish
mountains and saw, briefly, the blue waters of Barcelona.

Elspeth in the Garden

She inspected the blossom in the dark
in the hour before dawn, when the night
was at its coolest, before birdsong, before
the air's cold tremor gives way
to the breathless smile of morning.
Surely, she stepped across the flowerbeds,
outside the railway carriages she made
her home, where the blooms filled
the window boxes, like handkerchiefs
held out to the wind by day trippers.
The tulips were hushed, a blushing assembly.
They waited for her instructions.
She felt the tug of grass around her ankles
and thought of October, when the pumpkins
would rest their heads on the earth.
Her black coffee reflected the night,
stirred by the steel ripple of the moon.

At the bottom of the garden she met
the ghost of herself, who told her to go
back to bed, back inside where her
lurcher was curled up on the rug, books
were stacked beneath the piano stool
and Bob Dylan slept on his sleeve,
his tangled hair in his hands.

The sea listened to her footsteps;
stars scattered like seeds across the sky.
The birdbox was empty, the lantern
burned black on the garden table,
but even then, she could make out
the white bloom of a star magnolia
outstretched like a bride for her husband.
Beyond, a huddle of daffodils stared
like passengers on the opposite platform,
beckoning for her to cross the line.

Charlotte Brontë in the Wild West

'What suggested the Wild West to your mind, Miss Keeldar?'
                                        - Charlotte Brontë, *Shirley*

Still light outside but in the dark
of this midday saloon, you sit
at the bar with your pens and ink
and an untouched glass of vermouth.
In the corner, Mr Rochester leans into
a card game, his spurs spinning at his heels.
Somewhere on the hill Emily is teaching
poetry to a tribe of Sioux Indians while
Branwell drowns his promise in blue gin.
Anne coughs in the full moon of a Texan sun.

This could just as easily be the Fleece Inn,
outside, the cobbled streets of Haworth,
with rain on the Pennines instead of the Rockies.
Your Wild West were the fells and dales
of Yorkshire, wet roses and wild horses,
where the sun rises like a gold ingot
on the brow of the moors. Night falls,
and as you finish your chapter, a herd of bison
moves across the plain; above the desert,
a first of diamonds scatter to the wind.

The Small Ghost of Soho

Farewell then Dudley Moore,
giant of the diminished seventh, you taught
swinging London the meaning of jazz.
Your flat was a blizzard of white shirts,
each worn for a day then discarded.
They collected in drifts against the door
among miniskirts; your braces
dangled from a lover's foot.

That winter the jazz played on,
My Blue Heaven, *Indiana*, *Sad One for George,*
brandy on top of the piano,
you heard the ticking of the drum
and the footsteps of the bass
as it made its way down Dean Street.
In an empty room, there's a cloth cap
on a bedpost, while outside,
the rain falls like fingers on piano keys.
It dampens the sheets of the small ghost
that haunts Soho like a tune
you can't get out of your head.

Mappa Mundi

I drew the world on the back of cow
my inspiration the open window
I supposed a great ocean in the heavens
and a blue river that ran to the moon.
I worked mainly at dusk when the soft
light fell on the skin.

From my room, I could see the Tree of Paradise
the Nile and the golden domes of Jerusalem.
The monks ground ink for my land and sea
while I made a home for India's five thousand cities.
I questioned every visitor we had,
wringing them for news.

I placed Noah's Ark close to the Sea of Galillee.
Where I knew nothing, my hand
was guided by God; my pens produced islands,
rivers like serpents, tributaries
like the horns of a bull and Britain,
curled up like a new born babe.

I made homes for great tribes of the Earth,
like the Phanessi who wrapped their ears
around themselves against the cold.
I sketched the Sciapod crossing continents on his

single enormous foot. I searched the horizon
for glimpses of heaven.

When I had finished, I saw an eye peering
back at me: a world looking out on a world.
I took the hide to wise men; showed them
the round Earth and the short path
from Lincolnshire to Eden,
not a hundred day's north.

When winter came, I wrapped myself
in the map; I felt the world on my shoulders
while the cold sun dawned like gold leaf on Africa.
The Red Sea crept like a blood stain
from the calf that laid down
its life for the Earth.

The Underwater Ballerina

I swam between Houdini
and the vanishing elephants,
the greatest star in all of vaudeville.
I fell in love with America
in eight thousand gallons of water.
In this rising glass tank
I dance the Nutcracker
for gangsters in limelight.
Clad in gold, I am like
a mermaid that's bathed
in sunken treasure.
Beneath, I am wearing
the one-piece bathing suit
that scandalised a nation.

Some nights I see my sister's
face pressed against the glass.
When I swim, I think of a hundred
dollar bills floating on the surface
like Monet's water lilies.
Applause electrifies the tank
like rain on the sea.
But when I burst out
I am in Australian sunlight,
in my seventies, doing backstroke:

the Sugar Plum Fairy
on a turquoise ocean.
I see Houdini in the wings,
his arms folded, shaking his head,
wondering how I did it.

The Hill

And then, when it is almost time,
you step out of your hospital bed and start up the hill.
When you first look down,
the valley fills with sunlight like water in a basin.
On the brow of the opposite hill, you see yourself
as an altar boy in red and white cassocks,
your arms outstretched, impersonating
the *Christo Rei* above Rio de Janeiro.
On the lower roads, you wave on offers of lifts
from yellow Fiat 500s; *Old man,* they say,
you should not be out walking in the mountains.
In a shallow stream, you see your grey hair
has darkened to brown, your hands do not tremble.
As you climb higher, you are stronger still
and take the road in long strides. Monastery bells ring out.
You cross a dried stream and a path of violet flowers
and come to the house you grew up in.

You push open the door and find it empty
except for the upright piano and a photograph
of your idiot brother face down on the floor.
Now you are above the clouds; at the roadside
your father waves to you in the black waistcoat
he wore that day he left you at the seminary at 19.
You hear the bark of a deer in the woods

and come to a fork in the road where you find a crucifix
and a bucket of water. In the shadow of a broken barn,
you find yourself kissing a woman. You stop at streams
to look for newts and skip stones along the path;
staring up at the blue sky, it is easy to think of nothing.
Finally, as a child, barefoot, you step out of your clothes
and race the last stretch to the summit. Now you leap,
enclose the moon in your hand, cry out once, and disappear.

The Butcher of Florence

The play opens in the *Piazzo del Duomo*
beneath the skullcap of the cathedral
with an argument between a juggler and a jeweller.
The scene is incomplete, but we assume
these two have history; they leave a trail
of blood, pearls and burning torches.
A carriage of nobles arrives en route to the coast;
it is the youngest daughter's birthday
and both the juggler and the jeweller
are summoned to amuse her. There is something
about a storm and a medieval football match.

Shakespeare, it is thought, lost interest
in the play having developed a taste for Italian wine.
The manuscript was found sealed
inside a four hundred year old bottle of Chianti.
We know nothing of the butcher,
nor the fate of the juggler, but the daughter
we think, married the jeweller from the last surviving line:
*Her earrings were cast in light – they were
the last star of morning and the first star of night.*

r

ing of the frozen fens,
you etched your name into history.
Arms loose at your sides, you swept unchallenged,
like a cold wind across the marshes.
Beneath white skies you set your sights
on the island of Ely fastened to the horizon,
the sun smeared like butter across the ice.
Come race day, the brass band thundered,
frost on the tubas, while the bobbies
weaved through the crowds. Only
Gutta-Percha could touch you, as you swung
round the barrel, like a slingshot around the sun.
You held banisters of air; glided on invisible rails.
Diviner of balance and speed, fearless voyager
of the ephemeral, you clipped frozen ears
of grass, all the world a mirror beneath you.
Deep below were the Romans and fen men.
Crossing the finishing line, you skimmed
the nose of Guthlack, the early Christian hermit
preserved in the ice, his eyes closed in prayer.
When you knew the day was yours,
you heard the applause of lapwing and snipe
while Susan waited with your coat.
She made you supper of eel, pike and local ale.
That night, they toasted you from March
to Deeping and in your bed, dreaming, you
sailed into heaven on the edge of a diamond.

H.G. Wells Crash Lands in a Field in Suffolk

Out on a run,
I see a perfect sphere burning in the sky:
a nineteenth century balloon, losing height
and flickering like a Chinese lantern.
It comes down among the trees.
He steps out of the basket unscathed,
his moustache slightly singed,
a bare knee peeking through his spats.
Clapping the dust from his hands
he throws clear his leather satchel.
He greets me like an old friend,
shrugging at the wreckage behind him.
A primitive contraption, he explains,
restricted by the science of its age.
Tell me, are we far from Woking?
I take him into town, where he is mistaken
for an old country doctor; he peers
at the strange cars, the automatic
gates of the police station and the colour
television through the pub window.
Eventually, he speaks. *The Woking I know,*
I expect, is no longer the Woking it was.
Afraid to take him home, I call at Nick's house.
We make tea and invite him to play
Hot Shot's Golf on the PlayStation.

He is surprisingly good. Next we show
him the internet, taking care to explain
it all to him in advance. *As I expected,*
he says, settling down, requesting
a match for his pipe, *the Idea of*
A Permanent Encyclopaedia; we
leave him for a moment and when
we return, the wind blows the curtain
in on an empty room. On the screen, we read:
H.G.Wells: *About 1,950,000 results.*

After the Auction

I am the man who sold his life at auction,
who in good judgement gave up his best and worst;
threw in the town house, the servant and the top hat
won from a man on the train to Dawlish.

I disposed where I had once acquired:
cast off when once I called in:
my shares in the atmospheric railway,
a complete collection of *Punch*
and middle C from the family piano.

If I felt any attachment to my phonograph,
the bathing machine or my ten percent stake in the ferry
across the Exe, at that moment I felt none.
To the new owner of my high wire and balancing bar,
my officer's moustache from the Crimea
which I kept in a jar, I wish nothing but luck.

Into this bargain, I include an introduction
to each of my friends – Bartley, the surgeon;
Hargreaves, the botanist; Frederick the bohemian:
as hardy a club as any fellow could wish for.
If I should miss any of this, it would be
the first drink of the afternoon; our first rubber of whist.

To you I say this: treasure my Oxford Blue,
my Penny Black, the children playing tuba in the park,
the sound in my head when I cracked toffee
on the heating pipes at my grandfather's house;
the plimsolls in which I slipped down the stones
to the beach where I saw the other boy alone,
skimming rocks angrily into the sea.
Do not let this memory fade.

When you return to my wife, liberate my whisky
and best jokes; hang your hat on the bronze bust of my father,
think on this: be cautious with your cards;
I was the other boy; you are the other man.

The Whisperings

*i.m. William Wells b. 8 June 1919 d. 29 May 2001 and
Frederick Wells b. 8 June 1919 d. 8 June 1919*

You counted each other's fingers in the dark
faces pressed gently together, two brothers
asleep in the same bed; outside were the whisperings
like trees brushing against the window, the cow-moan
of your parents' voices while they chose names:
the engine driver with his black fingernails
and the housewife who pressed the bedclothes.

She held you both through her apron,
and looked out at the Ash tree in the garden;
felt the miracle of your elbows, your bird-boned arms.
and the flick of your eyelashes; synchronised swimmers,
you listened to the murmur of the amniotic world,
sensed the warmth of the other, and stared
through the blood water. You broke in a wave.

Born on the same day, you lived, Fred died:
two handfuls of sugar, held in the balance.
That morning was clear, bright; it rained in the afternoon.
You blinked in the sodium, an empty cot beside you.
His ghost aged with you, walked behind you on your
first day at school and dressed with you on your
wedding day as you parted your hair in the mirror.

He did not feel the sun on his face or taste
the salt on the wind, but nor he feel the loneliness
of the womb or miss a brother's accidental kiss.
You knew your sibling's secret, and shared
all the understanding of the dark. All your words
were unspoken. You had no picture, no photograph of him,
and no memories except the memory of love.